RAVEL

VALSES NOBLES ET SENTIMENTALES

FOR THE PIANO

EDITED BY MAURICE HINSON

AN ALFRED MASTERWORK EDITION

Second Edition
Copyright © MCMXCVIII by Alfred Publishing Co., Inc.
All rights reserved. Printed in USA.

Cover art: A detail from the portrait of Maurice Ravel
by Ludwig Nauer
Oil on canvas, 1930, Russia
Archiv für Kunst and Geschichte, Berlin

2

CONTENTS

FOREWORD

*We should always remember that sensitiveness and emotion
constitute the real content of a work of art.*

Maurice Ravel

The performance of a musical work places the pianist and the score in successively overlapping and cumulative roles. Progressing from symbol to experience, the score becomes ever more passive as the pianist becomes more active. At first the score attracts the pianist and then brings him back again and again even after it has been learned. During this period of assimilation, the pianist has increasing impact upon the score as his understanding of it grows and as he permeates it with his personal contribution.

The score is only an approximation of the composer's intentions. To represent it again by verbalizing removes it in yet another way from its essential and primary intent. But it is necessary to engage in this activity, especially in a work like the *Valses nobles et sentimentales* that has a sound-structure different from any other of Ravel's works, as well as from that of any other composition. Analysis will help show the *Valses* to be far more than a series of pieces organized on the surface by rhythmic and motivic elements, but one in which the substrata of compositional techniques serve as formalizing, unifying elements. Investing time in the understanding of these principles should prove rewarding for the inquiring pianist who is interested in arriving at a stylistically correct interpretation.

The pianist is constantly encouraged to refer to the score in order to draw the analysis into perspective with its aural context.

Context in Which the *Valses nobles et sentimentales* Was Written

Valses nobles et sentimentales appeared after a century of waltzes (the 19th) but it belongs to our century (the 20th). It was composed at a critical time in the music world, during the same years as *Le Sacre du Printemps* and *Pierrot Lunaire*. If one compares those innovative works of Stravinsky and Schoenberg to the *Valses,* it is evident that Ravel is similar in shedding some romantic tendencies. Ravel's masterpiece is like a kite being blown about in the winds of atonality yet held firmly by the tonal string. Today we do not hear irritating dissonance blocking otherwise lovely sound, but rather virile tone-combinations tempered and offset by more pliant harmonies, and we admire the bold freshness of this work written so early in the 20th century. There is no such thing any longer as an inadmissible chord, or melody, or rhythm—given the proper context, of course. Contemporary practice has firmly established that fact.

In the spring of 1910, a group of composers, most of them pupils of Gabriel Fauré, decided to set up a new musical organization in opposition to the *Societé Nationale de Musique.* The views of this new society were to be more liberal than the more traditional organization. Fauré was elected president of this new group and Ravel was one of the founders of the *Societé Musicale Indépendante.*

The *Valses nobles et sentimentales* had just been completed when the Committee of the S.M.I. decided, during 1911, to give a concert in which various works should be introduced to the public without any indication of the composer. Ravel commented:

The title, *Valses nobles et sentimentales* . . . sufficiently indicates that I was intent on writing a set of Schubertian waltzes. The virtuosity which was the basis of *Gaspard de la Nuit* has been replaced by writing of obviously greater clarity which has strengthened the harmony and sharpened the contrasts . . . The *Valses* were first performed to the accompaniment of hoots and cat-calls at the concert of the S.M.I., where the music was all anonymous. The audience voted for a possible composer of each piece. By a minute majority, the paternity of the *Valses* was ascribed to me . . .[1]

The identity of the composers had been kept so secret that not even the members of the Committee had known except where it was unavoidable. As for the *Valses,* only Louis Aubert knew the secret, since he was the pianist at this memorable concert and the work was dedicated to him in recognition of his talent as a pianist, as well as his being a good friend. Many of the professional musicians—and critics—appeared unimpressed by the *Valses.* Some of them identified the composer as Zoltán Kodály, Théodore Dubois, or Erik Satie. Few if any of those in the audience guessed who the composer was, and Ravel had to listen to the most ferocious criticism from friends who had no suspicion that he was actually the one who had written the offending music. Through the following hullabaloo Ravel made no particular response. Later, when the critics discovered who had written the *Valses*, they revised their judgement and found qualities they had failed to discover at the first hearing. This experience proved a lesson to Ravel in the true value of criticism.

The subtle harmonies of the *Valses nobles et sentimentales* elicited this comment from Claude Debussy: "It is the product of the finest ear that has ever existed." Although Schubert wrote several sets of waltzes, including the *Valses sentimentales* Op. 50 and the *Valses nobles* Op.77, there are no discernible musical contacts between Ravel and Schubert. It is quite possible that Ravel was inspired simply by the poetic sound of the titles. In any event, the titles are not unique to Schubert; Schumann, one of Ravel's youthful idols, had also written a *Valse noble* in his *Carnaval*.

If there is one influence in Ravel's *Valses nobles et sentimentales*, it is the Vienna of Johann Strauss, rather than that of Schubert. Especially in the seventh waltz, which Ravel claimed to be the most characteristic, the lilt, melodic line and the dramatic *tenuto* (measure 59), are more closely linked to the musical world of Strauss than to the rustic naiveté of Schubert (see Example 1).

Example 1
Waltz No. 7, measures 57–61

While the Schubert waltzes are, of course, completely tonal and, with one exception, in the major mode, the Ravel *Valses nobles et sentimentales* display major, minor, and modal scales and even polytonality. The simple waltz accompaniment of the Schubert pieces is replaced by Ravel with complex and varied rhythmical figures. The *Épilogue* in the Ravel work summarizes many elements drawn from the preceding seven pieces; this device was not used by Schubert, nor is there any similarity in form. In *Valses nobles et sentimentales* the predominant form is the expanded **A B A**; in Schubert's waltz collection the individual pieces are so short as to consist, in some cases, of only two or three phrases.

In addition to the Straussian elements mentioned above, there are also some Chopinesque features in the *Valses nobles et sentimentales*. The rhythmic device illustrated in Example 2 is obviously derived from the Chopin *Waltz* in A flat major, Op. 42, and the *Scherzo* in E major, Op. 54.

Example 2
Waltz No. 7
measure 67

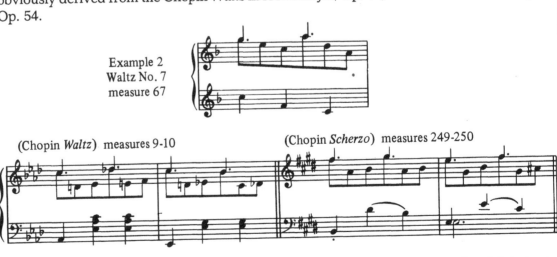

Actually it is not surprising to find the lack of any relationship between Ravel and Schubert. There is no evidence to support the claim that Ravel was an ardent admirer of Schubert or, for the matter, of any of the Viennese classicists with the exception of Mozart. The similarity of titles is the only link between the works in question.

Henri de Régnier, the poet whose lyrics had been the inspirational source for Ravel's *Jeux d'eau*, is quoted again at the beginning of the *Valses nobles et sentimentales*. The quotation reads ". . . le plaisir délicieux et toujours nouveau d'une occupation inutile" (the delicious and ever new pleasure of a useless occupation). Ravel's high spirits and pleasure-loving sophistication are well matched in the *Valses nobles et sentimentales*.

In its orchestral version, the title of the *Valses nobles et sentimentales* was changed to *Adélaïde ou la Langage des Fleurs* and a ballet scenario was written by Ravel himself. The ballet was produced by Mme. Natacha Trouhanova, whose *concerts de danse* included interpretations of classical and modern works.

Since the story of *Adélaïde* was created by Ravel to illustrate his own music, it is useful for the performer to become acquainted with the plot. The action takes place in the Paris salon of a courtesan named Adélaïde around 1820. There are seven scenes and an epilogue, as in the original piano version.

Scene 1   While the couples are waltzing or engaged in tender conversation, Adélaïde comes and goes. She is wearing a tuberose (a fragrant, white flower), the symbol of sensual pleasure.

Scene 2   Enter Lorédan in a melancholy mood. He offers her a buttercup, and the exchange of flowers that follows symbolizes Adélaïde's pretended affection and her suitor's love for her.

Scene 3   Adélaïde sees from the flower offered her that Lorédan's love for her is sincere, but the marguerite (a daisylike flower) she gave to Lorédan tells him that his love is not returned. Lorédan tries a second time, and this time the reply is favorable.

Scene 4   The lovers dance together affectionately, but are interrupted by the entrance of the Duke.

Scene 5   The Duke presents Adélaïde with a sunflower (a symbol of empty riches) and a diamond necklace, which she puts on.

Scene 6   Lorédan in despair presses his suit, but is repulsed flirtingly.

Scene 7   The Duke begs Adélaïde to give him the last waltz. She refuses, and goes in search of Lorédan who strikes an attitude of tragic despair. Finally he yields to her insistence and they go off together.

Epilogue   The guests retire. The Duke, hoping to be asked to stay, receives from Adélaïde's hands a branch of acacia (symbol of Platonic love) and departs in high dudgeon (angrily). Lorédan approaches looking very sad. Adélaïde gives him a poppy (an invitation to forget), but he rejects it and goes off, bidding her farewell forever. Adélaïde goes to the window and breathes the scent of the tuberose. Suddenly Lorédan appears on her balcony in a state of agitation, falls on his knees and presses a pistol to his head. But Adélaïde smilingly produces from her corsage a red rose and falls into his arms.[2]

Those who are familiar with the world of opera will notice a striking resemblance between this story and the plot of Giuseppe Verdi's *La Traviata* based upon the novel and play *La Dame aux camélias* by Alexander Dumas *fils*.

Organization of the *Valses nobles et sentimentales*

Because of the enormous melodic variety and harmonic diversity, plus rhythmic vitality far beyond what might be assumed from the three-four waltz meter, each waltz has a distinct personality. Individual use of expression marks and different types of sonorities create a finely tuned mood for the separate waltzes and the terms "noble" and "sentimental" do not nearly cover the emotional range.

The waltzes as a group have been termed "cyclic" because of the immediately recognizable quotations of a few melodies from earlier waltzes in the last one, the *Épilogue*. They are unusually full of transformed materials that are unifying elements on all compositional levels. Since one does not usually listen analytically to the waltz form, these elements tend to remain subliminal. The organizing factors within each waltz tend to be more immediately obvious to the ear than the shared content which integrates the whole set.

Ravel uses the two-measure group as the basic building block, and units are usually constructed in accumulated multiples of the basic two. Phrases and cadences clearly define both small and large sections. Recapitulation in each piece is an outstanding organizational aspect. Sections in each waltz are rarely delineated by new thematic materials; rather, the first exposed material is subjected to a reworking, from simple thematic variation (often combined with harmonic digression) to complex and vigorous development.

Formal Analysis

The first waltz is in **A B A** form and is in the key of G major. The **A** (exposition) section extends from measures 1–20; the **B** (development) section begins at measure 21 and ends at measure 60; section **A** (recapitulation) resumes at measure 61.

The first two measures include violent tone clusters, or unresolved discords. Actually, the first chord is an enharmonic dominant 13th. Its resolution in measure two is a G major (tonic) triad with added second (A) and sixth (E). The opening two measures, Ravel stated, consist of a linear progression, E sharp (beats one and two), to F sharp (beat three) to G (prolonged through measure two). The vigorous activity of the unresolved appoggiaturas sets the tone of this incisive waltz. Following the introductory measures 1–4, there is a balanced 16 measure phrase that modulates to and cadences in the key of the dominant, D major. The development section (**B**) (measures 21–60) uses thematic material from the exposition set in a bold manner involving considerable chromatic harmony. The recapitulation (measures 61–80) is the same length of the exposition (**A** section) and contains the same thematic materials in the same order.

The second waltz, a fragile and beautiful piece, sentimental and somewhat nostalgic, uses many augmented triads, and unfolds thematically and harmonically in sonatina form laced with the *ritornello* idea. The sectional form includes an introduction, measures 1–8, and a binary pattern (section **A** from measures 9–24, and section **B** from measures 25–32). This form is then repeated (introduction in measures 33–40; **A** from 41–56; and **B** from 57 to the end). The melodic section in part **A** is built on the Aeolian mode beginning on D. The indication *rubato* (measure 25) appears rarely in Ravel's scores. This waltz is among Ravel's very best works.

The third waltz is also in the Aeolian mode, this time beginning on E. The form of the third waltz is **A**: measures 1–16; **B**: 17–56; **A**: 57–72. The rhythmical pattern in measures 17–20 is in a triple pattern, while this pattern is changed in measures 25–28 to duple. This piece continues without stopping to the fourth waltz, and in measures 48–51 the rhythmical pattern of the fourth waltz is anticipated. The return of **A** in G major at measure 57 actually lasts only eight measures, but is extended and merges into a transition to the next waltz. The main theme sounds like a music-box tune.

The fourth waltz, like the second, is based primarily upon thirds and frequently utilizes hemiola rhythm. It has a strong Viennese character. The form is **A B A**. **A** extends from measures 1–16; **B** from measures 17–38, and the return **A** from measures 39 to the end. Thematic integration is more pronounced than in the third waltz, and the contrast at measure 17 is more one of register than of new materials. The pattern of thirds is not obvious until the repeat of section **A** where the descending chromatic line goes from D sharp to D natural, C sharp, etc. In the beginning this pattern is not as obvious because Ravel sustitutes an E natural for the D sharp and the D natural before beginning the progression. The tonality of the fourth waltz is quite ambiguous.

The fifth waltz, in E major, is like a slow interlude, sensuous and dreamlike. It is the shortest of the set (only 32 measures) and is also written in **A B A** form. The **A** section extends from measures 1–16; the **B** section ranges from measures 17–24; and the repeat of **A** is from measure 25 to the end, although it is not exactly like the opening. The Chopinesque waltz rhythm which Ravel used in the seventh waltz (illustrated in Example 3) is anticipated in measures 19–20 and 23–24 of the fifth waltz. Ravel wrote on Vlado Perlemuter's score of this waltz, "In the spirit of a Schubert Waltz." Ravel also wrote the word "simple" in the first measure.

The sixth waltz is in C major and it is the most monothematic of all. The basic melodic element of this piece from the beginning is a rising half-step progression. This is extended in measures 37–44 where the melody begins on B and rises to C, C sharp, D, D sharp, E, E sharp, F sharp, G, G sharp, and A. The form of the sixth waltz is **A B A**: **A**=measures 1–16; **B**=17–44; **A**=45–60. The **B** section is a variation of the **A** section, then goes into a development of its own material at measure 29 which also serves as a long transition to the **A** section that returns complete and intact.

The seventh waltz is by far the longest and most elaborate of the set. Ravel found it the "most characteristic" of the series, perhaps because it encompasses languid and brilliant moods coupled with the rhythmic hesitation of the Viennese waltz. After a brief introduction (measures 1–15) based on materials from the preceding waltz, the **A** section of this piece begins in measure 17 with a full blossoming tune, and continues to measure 66; it is later repeated without change from measures 111–158. The **A** section contains two thematic groups, one lyrical (measures 17–38), the other in that vein but gradually changing to a very dramatic character (measures 39–66). The **B** section (measures 66–110) is bitonal at times and contrasted thematically with the **A** section thematic material. In measures 68–69 the left hand is in F major while the right hand plays in E major. This procedure recurs frequently throughout the entire **B** section.

The *Épilogue* (Waltz No. 8) is among Ravel's finest inspirations and is based on melodic, rhythmic and harmonic elements of the previous seven waltzes. The form is **A B A**: **A** = measures 1–40; **B** = 41–61; **A** = 62–74. Measures 62–74 also serve as the coda. Important cadences are the demarcation points in the *Épilogue*. The sequence of reminiscences follow a mosaic pattern (the numbers below refer to the waltz number and number eight refers to melodic elements which appear only in the *Épilogue*: 8, 4, 8, 4, 8, 6, 8, 4, 1, 8, 6, 7, 6, 3, 4, 1, 8, 2.)

The musical ideas and moods of the *Valses* are woven into a fine and delicate ending in the *Épilogue*, where they are meshed with the harmony and tonality to form a rounded closing section. The *Valses*, as a group, are cyclic from the compositional standpoint, and the themes treated in the manner of an epilogue by use of the "flashback" technique.

The interpreter of the *Valses nobles et sentimentales* is urged to examine the score of the orchestral version in order to capture and reproduce some of the brilliant and colorful effects achieved by the composer.

Although Ravel occasionally analyzed his music on a chord to chord basis, he was also well aware of large structural sections, as is evident from his analysis of the following passage from the *Valses nobles et sentimentales*. "With regard to unresolved appoggiaturas," he wrote to René Lenormand, "here is a passage which may interest you."

Example 3
Waltz No. 7
measures 66-78

Example 4

This fragment is based upon a single chord (see Example 4), which was already used by Beethoven, without preparation, at the beginning of a sonata (Op. 31, No. 3).

Below is the same passage with the appogiaturas resolved, resolutions which really do not alter anything until the last measure in Example 3.

Example 5
measures 66-70

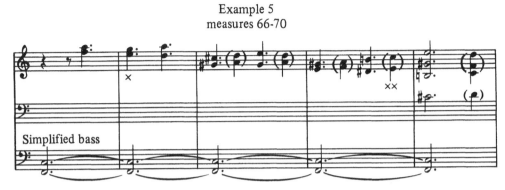

Simplified bass

"The E does not change the chord. It is a passing note in both cases." (See Example 6.) Arbie Orenstein. *Ravel: Man and Musician.* pp. 132–35.

Example 6

Performing the *Valses nobles et sentimentales*

Ravel made a recording of the *Valses* in 1913, originally on the Welte-Vorsetzer system. In the issue of this recording on Sony Superscope[3] there appears to be a serious defect in the re-processing of this recording to a long-playing record. In the recording the tempos are very different from Ravel's metronome markings, sometimes grossly so. There is always the remote possibility that Ravel did play these tempos on that particular occasion, but evidence against it is strong. The following shows the tempo of each waltz as indicated by Ravel in the score, those heard on the recording as far as it was possible to detect them by metronome despite fluctuations within each piece, and the percentage of differences:

Waltz	Score	Recording	Difference
1	176	108	46%
2	104	152	32%
3	modéré	92	
4	80	132	39%
5	96	132	27%
6	100	144	31%
7	moins vif	92–112	
8	76	92–104	27%

The time given for the complete *Valses* in the *Catalogue de l'oeuvre de Maurice Ravel,* published by Publie par les soins de la Foundation Maurice Ravel. Paris: Les Presses de L'impremerie Chaix, 1954, p. 37, is 14 minutes, 25 seconds. It is unknown how this figure was determined. In order to compare some other performances by well-known artists, Gieseking's recorded time is given as 13 minutes, Perlemuter's is 13 minutes, 57 seconds, and de Larrocha's is 14 minutes and 50 seconds.[4] Ravel's recorded performing time is 10 minutes and 32 seconds, an overall faster speed by 28%. An interesting comment on the fast tempo of Waltz No. 1 is made by Hélène Jourdan-Morhange and Vlado Perlemuter in the book *Ravel d'après Ravel*[5]: "Let us begin with the rhythm. Of course, it is less fast than one usually hears it played." Perlemuter—"Exactly. Ravel indicates the metronomic time, but it is necessary to keep it moving in a spirited but not disheveled way." The two artists agree that Waltz No. 1 is usually played too fast.

Ravel's interpretation of the *Valses* is full of the mannerisms one sometimes hears in the performance of "keyboard immortals"—uneven striking of the members of the chord, or outright rolling of chords although unmarked. This does not occur out of technical duress, because in Waltz No. 1, measures 17–18, the large chords with nine notes are played perfectly together, the right hand reaching a ninth with a note for every finger. Rather, it occurs where a stylized waltz pattern appears in the left hand. In Waltz No. 2 and similar places, the accompaniment of beats "two-three" is sometimes broken.

The already mentioned book *Ravel d'après Ravel* by Hélène Jourdan-Morhange and Vlado Perlemuter, is a valuable source concerning the performance practice of Ravel's piano works. Perlemuter was the first to give a performance of Ravel's complete piano works in two recitals in 1929, and the text of that book is drawn from a series of radio broadcasts in the format of interviews conducted by Mlle. Jourdan-Morhange during which Perlemuter takes the opportunity to play, discuss and give examples from all Ravel's piano works. Mlle. Jourdan-Morhange was a violinist and a close personal friend of Ravel's for many years, so the interview is a lively exchange between two privileged musicians who passed on many of Ravel's comments. Vlado Perlemuter had studied earlier with Cortot and Moskowski and still teaches (as of 1988) at the Paris Conservatory. His lessons with Ravel took place over a period of six months at the composer's Montfort – l'Amaury home (now a Ravel museum), about fifteen miles outside of Paris.

While the music of Debussy and Ravel seems occasionally to call for the use of the *sostenuto* pedal, the fact is that these composers did not write with it in mind but themselves used various types of partial pedaling with the damper. Their music was not the first with examples of "three-handed" playing since this appears liberally through the music of Beethoven, Schumann, Liszt, Brahms and others. In 1893, before Debussy and Ravel had written the main body of their piano music, Hans Schmitt, a very thorough pedagogue, mentions Steinway's *sostenuto* pedal and others of the time, but does not really indicate the conditions of their use. Rather, he suggested partial pedaling of the damper to solve the problems of layered sonorities.[6] In Ravel's recording of the *Valses*, the damper pedal is used to hold certain bass notes although the chords above cause blurring. He does not always hold the bass note for its full written value in these cases, but it is as if the written note were the theoretical underpinning of the section, to be understood by the listening ear. It is difficult to tell whether Ravel is attempting partial pedaling to erase upper tones but maintain the bass. Then too, bass notes are often held longer than their written values, again producing a certain amount of blending. These observations are, however, somewhat subjective because of the poor quality of the recording.

While pedaling is often mentioned in *Ravel d'après Ravel*, the sostenuto pedal is never suggested or mentioned. Perlemuter's lessons with Ravel took place after 1922, on Ravel's Érard grand which was not equipped with a sostenuto pedal. If Perlemuter had that pedal available during his radio broadcasts which are the basis for the book, it is not mentioned. Perlemuter does make the following references to the use of the pedal: "It was the first time Ravel had me really work out the pedal. He felt it essential for the *Valses* . . . In general, use pedalings that underline the rhythm."

A most interesting insight to pedaling practice comes not from the discussion of the *Valses*, but of the *Sonatine*. Mlle. Jourdan-Morhange asked about the ending of the second movement, where the bass note is to be held while both hands are occupied in the higher register with harmonies that move through the bass note.

Mlle. Jourdan-Morhange: "But how, without mixing the harmonies, do you maintain the pedal?"

Vlado Perlemuter:

> You underline them by a method that serves for Ravel's music as well as it does for that of Debussy: that is, a light vibration of the foot on the pedal, which if well done, allows the bass to remain, over which the extraneous harmonies glide. They fade delicately letting the fundamental vibrate to the end.

Abram Chasins also played for Ravel, and says:[7]

> Ravel, in response to certain pedal effects I had devised for his exquisite *Sonatine* exclaimed: 'Why didn't someone show me that such effects were possible with a sustaining pedal? How many more possibilities it would have suggested to me!'

In order to clarify the incident, Mr. Chasins has added the following:

> Ravel had never before encountered a sostenuto pedal. The effects I showed him might have been my own inventions, for they did indeed use all three pedals, but primarily the simultaneous depression of both the sostenuto and soft pedal with the left foot angled to accomplish that.[8]

Use of the Sostenuto Pedal

Surely Ravel would have taken advantage of the *sostenuto* pedal as a composer and performer if one had been at his disposal. It was his nature to explore the limits of the instruments for which he wrote. The orchestration of the *Valses* provides an interesting study concerning tonal layering at those places where the piano would necessarily produce a harmonic blur if only the damper pedal were used to sustain a bass note for its written value. Ravel does not attempt to orchestrate in such a blending, but allows each line to be distinct at chord changes. This fact should by no means be held up as an ideal for the piano version in an attempt to "orchestrate out" the mixed harmonies at every opportunity. There are many places where chromatic coloration is a part of the fabric and should in no way be pedaled out for a more "pure" sound. (See Waltz No. 4, measures 1–4.) Because of these places, the pianist should try for a more integrated over-all style by allowing some mixture of harmonies in other areas as well.

Evenness of Tone and Tempo

Ravel's statement, "It is enough to let my music express itself," is very pertinent for the *Valses*. Dynamic and expression marks are nearly always precisely placed and one carries over to the next without the need for interpolations beyond small nuances. The very best way to have certain sections sound is to play with the most even amount of tone possible. For example, in Waltz No. 7 beginning at measure 67, if one works to bring out the little contrapuntal line E, D, C-sharp (measures 67–68) and then E, D-sharp, C-sharp (measures 69–70) the music could become distorted. If an even amount of tone is used the notes will sound in a line and stand out by themselves.

Even more important is evenness of tempo. The waltzes are about motion and movement, not just superficially, but in their innermost workings. Movement is written into the piece and too much rubato destroys the inner rhythmic tensions. For example, in the first eight measure phrase of Waltz No. 3, the inner chromatic lines and the duple rhythm excite the phrase sufficiently and a tempo increase would make it difficult to resettle the phrase on E.

Pedaling and Articulation

Care in pedaling and observing the articulation slurs with which it is connected is perhaps the single most important factor for a stylistically correct interpretation. The pedal should never mask or cover the ends of slurs, except in special instances, when the damper must hold a bass note. The slurs are more a *legato* mark – they often indicate that the last note or notes are to be played more lightly. Since the slurs are often placed on beats two and three, they give the right amount of lilt to the music and make unnecessary any need for a tempo distortion to cause the three-four meter to pulse with that extra small amount on the first beats to indicate that the rhythm is a dance rhythm.

Ravel's pedal markings in Waltz No. 2 are the only ones in the whole work besides the markings for the *una corda* pedal in Waltz No. 8. At the same time, there are no fingerings indicated. The editor has tried to devise fine legato fingerings which will make the slur articulations meaningful and not always dependent upon the pedal for such connections.

Performance Suggestions for the *Valses*

Waltz No. 1 For measures 5 and 6, smaller hands should use two thumbs in a row on D-E. This is good because the E will get its full emphasis as accented passing tone and added sixth to the harmony. Keep the hemiola chords in measures 17 and 18 in strict time or the cross-rhythm is lost along with the upbeat feeling. Take the *sans ralentir* seriously. Ravel does hold back ever so slightly in his recording at this place without detriment. In measures 17 and 18 the chord span is a problem for some hands. There are several good solutions: (1) Hold the pedal through the rests to ease the strain. Only the first chord would have to be split; on the next two, the left hand B and the right hand G could be omitted, and those two notes, doubled in different octaves, would still be struck again, reactivating the strings on the already raised dampers of the omitted notes. (2) Play the left-hand A and the right-hand G together, then the remainder of the chord as rapidly as possible. This sounds best when the pedal is used. If a pedal is used across these beats, release it so beat one of measure 19 will be empty. For measures 33 and 34, the pressure tenuto is for the left hand only. The melody begins on the downbeat and the measure becomes distorted if both parts fall into the second beat. (Ravel begins the second beat a little early.) Here the two-beat slur placed in the last part of the measure is a guide to give more of the second beat and lift off the third. It is especially important to listen for the inner line, G-sharp, F-double-sharp, F-sharp, F-double-sharp, a restatement of the opening chromatic half-steps. Soon this line will expand, and become the basis for the chromatic voice-leadings in many other places. In measures 45–48, bring out the thumb side of the right hand on beats 1 and 2, and the top of each chord in beat three to emphasize the chromatic half-step binding the chords together. In measures 79–80 the *un peu pesante* requires a slight holding back to realize the heavy feeling, otherwise it is only louder.

Waltz No. 2 At measure 25 there is a rubato marking, which Ravel uses very infrequently. A description from one of his contemporaries, Hélène Jourdan-Morhange will be helpful at this point. She said the rubato in Ravel's music is always clear and easy to understand. Ricardo Viñes said that since Ravel loved precise interpretations, he invented just a 'dose' of rubato; a rubato in one specific place. Vlado Perlemuter commented that here, it is more like a waltz hesitation than a romantic rubato as in Chopin. The entire marking then, *au Mouvement (un peu plus lent et rubato)*, means the tempo is resumed after the *ralentir*, except that it is first affected by the rubato, which is not a give and take, but an evenly slow beat, faster than the previous *ralentir*, but slower yet than the original tempo. The tempo is resumed on the third beat of measure 26. Once again in measure 27 a sudden hesitation should be taken, probably not as much as the first time. This execution is supported in Ravel's recording. In measure 26 the second-beat C goes into the third-beat D. In measures 33–36 the melody can be heard moving up in a sequence of half steps. Ravel and Perlemuter both increased the tempo into beat three, measure 36, Ravel quite noticeably. The music intensifies here considerably at the climax of the melodic lines, to fall slowly into the recapitulation, and the increase does not seem misplaced. In measures 49–52, it may be necessary to divide the left-hand chord. A good solution is to play the lower G, B-flat, C-sharp on the beat, striking the upper B-flat immediately after; this B-flat then blends in well with the one on the second beat and is very close to the original intention. In measure 51 it is possible to take the upper B-flat with the right hand, thus striking that chord with all notes together.

Waltz No. 3 The tempo indication is *Modéré*. This should be faster than the previous waltz, but not at all rushed. The tempo should only have very subtle variations. The staccatos are important. Hold the second beat A in the right hand, measure 1, a little longer than the staccato in the left hand so the C-D pairs will sound as though they are separate from the rest of the texture. At measures 62 and 63, the ritard is written in. Only a very little holding back is necessary.

Waltz No. 4 At measures 31–36 the dynamic markings in this false recapitulation are different from any other phrase in the piece. Ravel (in performance) further enriches this section with an additional chromatic line taken from the orchestral version. He added it to Perlemuter's score during their study session:

Waltz No. 4, measures 31-37

Example 7

Waltz No. 5 Measures 1–4. The tempo change occurs in the performer's ear during the hold sign between the waltzes. At measures 9–12 melody notes should be more prominent when they sound against the double thirds of the accompaniment immediately below. At measure 25 the *sonore* marking is for the bass C-sharp to effect the modulation back to E.

Waltz No. 6 At measures 7 and 8, Ravel indicates a decrescendo immediately before the harmonic downbeat in measure 7. This is awkward unless a little pause is taken right before measure 7 – not a break in the sound but a tempo adjustment as if the *un peu languissant* were written one beat earlier. Measures 17–28 should be played very delicately and are difficult to do strictly in time. Lengthening of the beat between the phrase ending in measure 20 and its repetition (measures 21–22) is effective.

Waltz No. 7 In measures 1–15 it is important to keep the tempo strict so the syncopation will have meaning. The *languissant* in measure 9 will not be detrimental because the pattern is already established. Measures 31–38 should not be "too expressive," to allow the music to flow on into measure 39. At measure 43, Ravel does speed up from here to the climax at measures 59–66 but that is not necessary for a good line, nor is that really what *augmentez* means. [It means crescendo.] If the pianist simply builds the tone, the end point is actually more effective. At measure 66, there is no indicated pause before the next section opens, but a slight hesitation seems almost necessary, to clear the air of the A-major vibrations. Feel one beat per measure. At measures 100–110 keep the tempo strict so the cross-rhythms can be easily heard.

Waltz No. 8 (Épilogue) At measures 1–4, differentiate between the sixteenths and the grace note which is of undetermined value. The middle register melody notes G, F-sharp, E, F-sharp, should shine through. At measures 5 and 13 *sourdine* (*una corda* pedal) is marked when a melodic quotation enters and helps with the "drop-back" contrast for two measures. Measures 35–40: this cadence to the tonic in G is more dynamic, more drawn out than the cadence in B in measures 15–20, and should be more expressive. Measures 50–61: these measures must stay strictly in tempo except as marked so their proportions will be correct. At measure 60, Ravel indicates *staccato*, with extra pressure on each first note of the group. Measures 66–74 work better for the editor if the notes between the hands are redistributed. The purpose is to give more control over the grace-note octaves, and to get a more complete *legato* for the melody by never manually releasing the notes until the next one sounds.

Programming the *Valses nobles et sentimentales*

The *Valses* are introspective much of the time, and the ending is especially contemplative. There are other works in the repertoire for which the tradition of terminal applause seems quite unsuited, such as the Schumann *Kinderszenen*, Op. 15, and the Bartók *Suite*, Op. 14. Their placement at the end of a program is especially inappropriate because the audience usually wishes to applaud not only for the just completed work but for the artist and the entire program that was offered. Certainly the programming of two pieces or groups with prolonged quiet endings should be avoided.

That a programming difficulty exists is indicated by Jules van Ackere:

> The Épilogue ends on the theme of Waltz 2, in a surreal pianississimo [*ppp*]. After that, it is the practice of some pianists to repeat Waltz 7, wishing to end in a more lively mood. That is heresy which goes directly against the author's design.[9]

This would end the set in the key of A rather than the tonic G, needlessly repeat the materials of Waltz No. 7 which are already well developed, and do violence to the form.

Should one waltz be separated from the rest and played as an occasional piece or an encore? This is a good question, and we do have the precedent from Ravel in his other works. When in the United States, at least, he played separately the "Menuet" and "Rigaudon" from *Le Tombeau de Couperin* and "La Vallée des Cloches" from *Miroirs*. It would not be possible to separate Waltz No. 3 since it has no ending of its own. The middle Nos. 4, 5 and 6 are extremely short and need each other to balance their harmonic usage; then too, No. 6 has no good close because the final cadence is tonally rather indecisive, rather like the beginning. Waltz No. 8, without its predecessors, would be too much of an enigma. That leaves Nos. 1, 2 and 7 as possibilities for single performance.

Ravel felt strongly that the indication of each waltz (Modéré – très franc; Assez lent, etc.) should be listed on the printed program.

First page of the manuscript. Compare with page 16.

The piano compositions of Maurice Ravel belong, for me, to the most interesting works of piano literature. No other composer, including Debussy, has "instrumented" better for the two hands and pedals of pianists. If Debussy's creations are more varied and perhaps richer in expression, then Ravel has attained such unheard-of brilliance of style that it is futile to argue about who of the two great French masters (who, until now, remain unexcelled in 20th-century piano music) has created the most valuable works. For me, Debussy and Ravel signify the complete exploitation of the possibilities of the modern piano.

Liszt and several Russian composers draw great amounts of sonority from the instrument—this "noisy" kind of sound prohibits the delicacy and *"bon gout"* of the French masters—Scriabin and Rachmaninoff have often written an exemplary and beautiful-sounding piano movement. However, the absolute unity of inspiration and instrumental execution, the inventiveness

derived from the uniqueness of piano sound and the special possibilities of the piano have not happened to the same extent as with Debussy and Ravel.

Consider a piece such as the "Alborada del gracioso," which unfortunately, possibly because of its difficulties, is heard more often as an orchestral piece than in the original version for piano—anyway, Ravel has orchestrated it masterfully himself—or study "Ondine" or "Scarbo," these fairy tales and ghost stories from the *"Gaspard de la nuit:"* Is it not admirable to the greatest degree how an improbable richness of inspiration of highest pianistic brilliance and unrestrained sound-pleasure serves poetic-musical expression? Has complete mastery of conception as well as of composition created here a piano style which only serves as a vehicle for dazzling virtuosity and finger agility of the player or for his more or less external outbreaks of temperament? No, each pianistic effect is inseparably bound to the logical development

"**How Does One Perform Ravel's Piano Music?"**
by
Walter Gieseking
(Translated by Ronald E. Booth II)

14

and formal construction of the work and is, as a result, musically justified.

A good interpretation, which unites correctness and stylistic authority with delicacy and sensitivity and thereby brings all the beauty to fruition, yields the most magnificent tonal results. Naturally, such highly-developed music is not easy to perform, and the slow movements, which do not place such enormous demands for accuracy on the performer, are also never easy to perform, because they demand a far-reaching mastery of the finest nuances of touch.

Now, it is unique that some pianists instinctively use this differentiated touch and, in the same way, the correct use of pedal, while others who often are able to do much more technically confront impressionistic music in such a perplexed way that it remains without thought and sound under their hands. But through these "others" I have learned that problems are present here whose solution is not familiar to every pianist. I have never found it difficult to perform sonorously such fully-composed music, and my interpretations simply evolve from the self-evident necessity for me to play the piano so that it sounds beautiful.

Without a practical demonstration at the piano, it is difficult in a few sentences to describe, so-to-speak theoretically, a performance of the sound world of Ravel (and Debussy). Nevertheless, I will attempt to formulate some advice.

The clear interpretation of simple music is founded – roughly spoken – upon the confrontation of three components including melody, bass and harmonic filling (accompaniment) in the following levels of tonal intensity: Melody – loudest of all, bass – weaker, and harmony – subordinated. With contrapuntally-composed works the main subject (theme) appears in place of the melody, to which the answer or counter-subject and thereafter the thematically unimportant voices are subordinated. With the more richly elaborated works comes a growing number of neighboring voices which, from time to time, must be emphasized according to their importance. However, the harmony always remains limited to the chord-tones which belong to it.

The impressionists, who enrich harmony and also evoke the illusion of tonal color on the piano through the inclusion of distant "dissonant" overtones, make a far-reaching gradation of tonal intensity (i.e., loudness) within a chord necessary, especially if such chords contain essentially more tones than the conventional three or four. The correct tonal mixture results mostly if the consonant tones are sounded more strongly and the dissonant tones more softly – according to the extent of their relationship to the fundamental tone. Instead of a simple tonal gamut with increasing volume as main theme, secondary theme, bass and harmony, a single-functioning gradation of all tones of a chord connection becomes necessary whereby often one or more main voices or single important tones must stand out. Along with this, the entire tonal foundation must be given appropriate nuance ("– nuanciert werden muss –") according to the harmonic importance of each tone.

Especially important is the correct reverberation of the bass tones, which correspondingly must be clearly struck and sustained (mostly) with the pedal. Many fluctuating harmonies, where movement and change can be illogical if the fundamental of the root is missing, are accountable to the ear only in relation to the basses. Very often passages or chord sequences must be played so quietly that they fade away immediately when the next tones are struck, in spite of a raised damper. Naturally this is only feasible in the treble or possibly in the middle range of the piano, whereas bass progressions are connected with the use of pedal, as a rule.

The right pedal must be used a great deal and can often be held for a very long time (often an entire page with Debussy!). That all tones must be proportioned to each other in terms of loudness is self-evident.

To play a succession of melodic tones with raised damper pedal demands the most careful control of nuance, especially with a succession of descending tones. Each tone must, in this manner, cancel out the previous tone, which is achieved with a very careful, imperceptible crescendo and with an ascending melodic line this is, naturally, significantly easier. This fine gradation of sound must not assume the character of real accents because these must be saved for the places where the composer specifically demands them. With the French masters, performance indications must, in general, be observed most precisely; tempo changes and rubato playing, especially, are to occur only where they are indicated. The indications "cédez" and "serrez" ("holding back" and "tightening up") are mostly no more than "agogic" fluctuations used almost continually in the German-romantic style of interpretation. Except in places especially indicated, the tempo is, as a rule, the same (i.e., it does not change).

The performance of all these discrete nuances demands a refined touch which must be learned with the foundation of absolutely even and accurate playing. Whoever has not trained his fingers sufficiently in this evenness of touch will achieve this "colored" playing only in the fortunate exceptional cases where an especially sensitive ear has intuitively enabled the fingers to have a certain modulation of touch.

The pianist who masters his instrument in this manner will find the most beautiful opportunities in the piano works of Ravel to show his ability. The audiences of all countries will then listen to him thankfully, and there should be no pianist who does not know these masterworks.[10]

About This Edition and Series

The "Anatomy of a Classic" series is designed to help the pianist dissect and put together again the masterpiece that is presented. This series is intended to assist the performer in synthesizing many of his/her previous musical disciplines that may have been experienced as separate entities. By placing the work under discussion and analysis in its proper context with other compositions and events, the intelligent pianist should be better able to realize a more accurate stylistic performance.

At some point it is absolutely necessary for players to study the compositional process to realize a more correct performance. This editor believes that analysis is an indispensable part of preparation for performance.

I have used the first edition of *Valses nobles et sentimentales* (Durand et Fils, Paris, France, 1911) as the basis for this edition. Ravel's orchestrated version of the work, also printed by Durand, was used on a comparative basis for the present edition.

Ravel's pedal indications are identified in footnotes and have been incorporated into the editor's pedaling. All fingering and marks in parentheses are editorial. "U. C." implies use of the *una corda* (soft) pedal. "T. C." (*tre corde*, or three strings), is used to cancel the *una corda*, so that all strings are struck by the hammer. "SOS" indicates use of the *sostenuto* pedal. "Up SOS" indicates release of this pedal.

The editor hopes that this performing, analytical, and teaching edition will help the pianist to understand more clearly some of Ravel's creative processes, and introduce him/her to one of the composer's masterpieces.

This edition is dedicated to Nancy Bricard,
with admiration and appreciation.

Maurice Hinson

Sources Consulted in the Preparation of this Collection

Norman Demuth. *Musical Trends in the 20th Century.* London: Rockliff, 1952.

Stelio Dubbiosi. "The Piano Music of Maurice Ravel: An Analysis of the Technical and Interpretative Problems Inherent in the Pianistic Style of Maurice Ravel." Dissertation, New York University, 1967.

Madeline Goss. *Bolero—The Life of Maurice Ravel.* New York: Tudor Publishing Co., 1945.

Elizabeth McCrae. "Ravel's *Valses nobles et sentimentales*: Analysis, Stylistic Considerations, Performance Problems." Dissertation, Boston University, 1974.

Arbie Orenstein. *Ravel: Man and Musician.* New York: Columbia University Press, 1975.

Endnotes

[1] Madeline Goss. *Bolero. The Life of Maurice Ravel.* New York: Tudor Publishing Co. 1940, pp. 159–60.

[2] Rollo H. Myers. *Ravel, Life and Works.* New York: Thomas Yesoloff, 1960, pp. 170-1.

[3] Maurice Ravel. *Great Composers Play Their Own Works in Stereo,* Keyboard Immortal Series 4–AO 72-3 #9. Sony Superscope, Sun Valley, California, 1970.

[4] Walter Gieseking. *Maurice Ravel, Complete Works for Piano Solo,* Angel 35272, Side 1, Band 4. Vlado Perlemuter. *The Complete Piano Music of Maurice Ravel,* Vox SVBX 5410, Side 5, Band 5. Alicia de Larrocha. *Ravel,* Columbia M 30115, Side 1, Band 2.

[5] Editions du Cervin, Lausanne, Switzerland, 1957. "5me édition et augmentée." N.B.: in this 5th edition Perlemuter added two chapters on the piano concertos which he did not study with Ravel. There also exists a Japanese translation.

[6] Hans Schmitt. *The Pedals of the Piano-Forte.* Philadelphia: Theodore Presser, 1893, tr. Frederick Law.

[7] Abram Chasins. *Speaking of Pianists.* New York: Alfred A. Knopf, 1961, p. 76.

[8] Elizabeth McCrae. "Ravel's *Valses nobles et sentimentales*: Analysis, Stylistic Considerations, Performance Problems." Diss., Boston University, 1974, p. 153.

[9] Jules van Ackere. *Maurice Ravel.* Bruxelles: Elsevier, 1957, p. 35.

[10] This article appeared in *Melos,* December 1947, p. 412.

Valses nobles et sentimentales
(Noble and Sentimental Waltzes)
ADÉLAÏDE

". . . le plaisir délicieux
et toujours nouveau d'une
occupation inutile."

Henri de Régnier
(. . . the delicious and ever new
pleasure of a useless occupation.)

MAURICE RAVEL
(1875–1937)

I

(Moderate-very straight forward)
Modéré-très franc ♩ = 176

(With no ritard.)
Sans ralentir

II

(Rather slowly—with great feeling)
Assez lent—avec une expression intense ♩ = 104
en dehors (in the foreground—bring out)

A tempo
doux et expressif (gently and expressive)

ⓐ Grace notes should be played slightly before the beat.

ⓑ Ravel indicated pedal at measure 31, second beat.

© Ravel's parentheses.

ⓓ Ravel indicated pedal at measure 63, second beat.

III

© Editor's suggested metronome indication.

IV

V

(Almost slow—with an intimate feeling)
Presque lent—dans un sentiment intime ♩ = 96
le chant très en dehors (the melody well brought out)

VI

VII

① Editor's tempo suggestion.

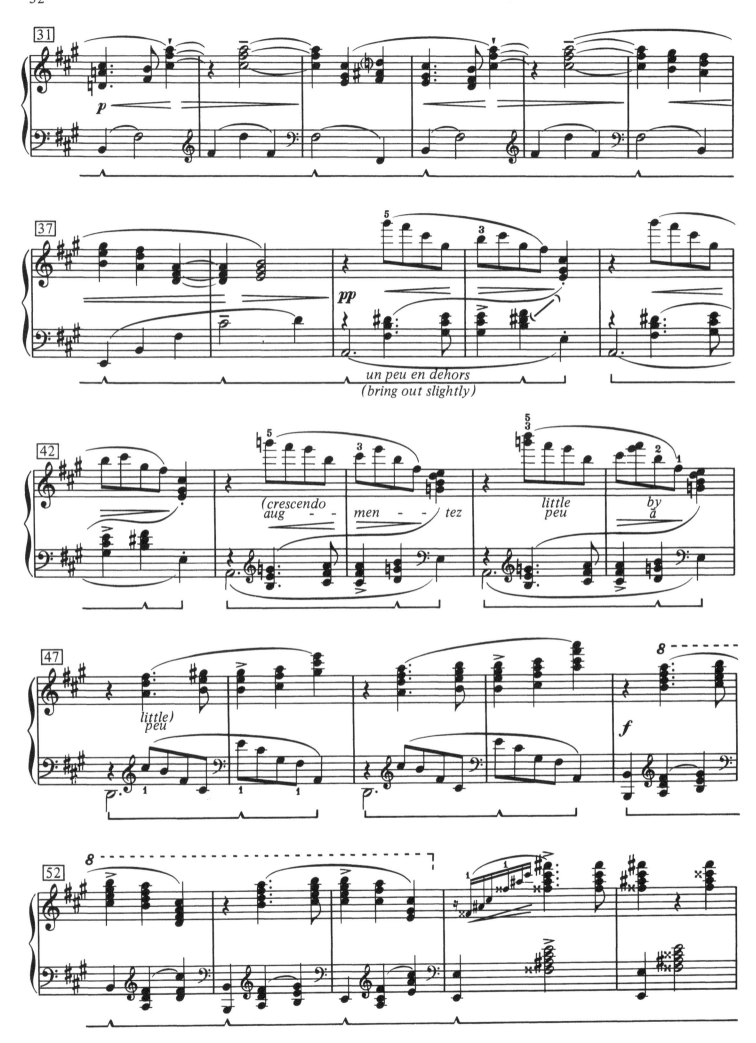

VIII

ÉPILOGUE (Conclusion)
(Slow)
Lent ♩ = 76

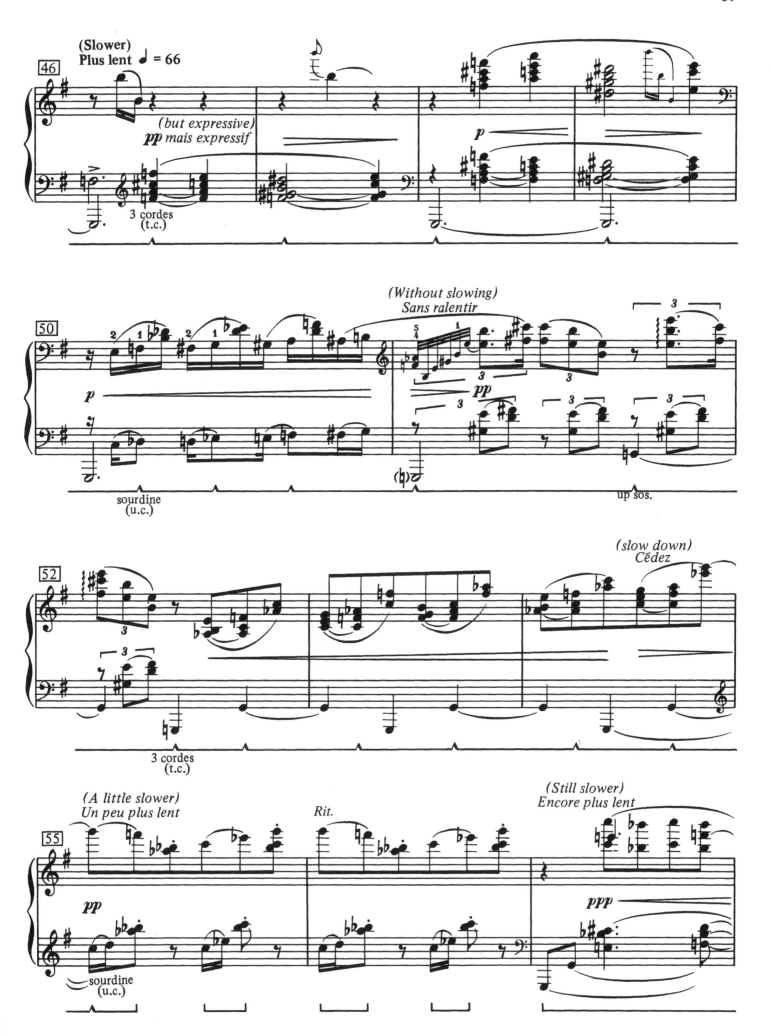